The Lit...

The Little Book of Rules

How to capture the heart of Mr Right

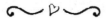

Thorsons

An Imprint of HarperCollins*Publishers*

Thorsons
An Imprint of HarperCollins*Publishers*
77–85 Fulham Palace Road,
Hammersmith, London W6 8JB

Published by Thorsons 1998

1 3 5 7 9 10 8 6 4 2

© Ellen Fein and Sherrie Schneider

Ellen Fein and Sherrie Schneider assert the moral
right to be identified as the authors of this work

A catalogue record for this book
is available from the British Library

ISBN 0 7225 3786 7

Printed in Great Britain by
Redwood Books, Trowbridge

Introduction

'The Rules' has become not just a bestselling book, but a phenomenon, revolutionizing dating practices around the world.

Why all the fuss? The answer is simple: 'The Rules' works! Unlike other dating books that give warm 'n' fuzzy, meaningless and misleading advice that doesn't work in real life – such as 'be yourself, don't play games, tell a man how you feel' – 'The Rules' tells the truth about dating and capturing the heart of Mr Right.

'The Rules' takes the analysis and angst out of dating. It's simple. If he calls you, he likes you. If he doesn't, Next!

Follow 'The Rules' and the man of your dreams will fall head over heels in love with you and before you know it you'll be marching down the aisle!

Men love a challenge –
don't make it easy
for them!

~ ♡ ~

Treat the men you want like the
men you don't want.

Tell yourself: 'Any man would be lucky to have me.'

Be mysterious. Leave a man hungry for more, not bored.

Act as if you were born happy.

How to act on dates one,
two and three...

☆ act nonchalantly as if you're
always on dates

☆ laugh at his jokes

☆ don't profess love to him
during dessert

If you're feeling nervous, pretend you're a movie star. Hold your head high and walk as if you just flew in from New York on Concorde.

Look feminine – you're dressing for
men, not other women.

♡

Don't leave the house without
wearing make-up.

Put lipstick on even when you go jogging.

Spray on an intoxicating perfume.

Don't behave like a man, even if you are head of your own company.

Always act ladylike, cross your legs
and smile.

♡

Wear fashionable, sexy clothes in bright colours.

Be a 'creature unlike
any other'.

Make your movements fluid and
sexy, not jerky or self-conscious.

Don't get your hair cut short –
we're girls, so why do we want to
look like boys!

Don't talk to a man first – wait for him to talk to you.

Men prefer long hair – it gives them something to play with and caress.

Wear black sheer stockings and hike up your skirt – this **really** entices the opposite sex!

How often are you
allowed to see him?

☆ first month: no more than once
or twice a week
☆ second month: no more than two
or three times a week
☆ third month: no more than four
or five times a week.

If he wants to see you seven days
a week...
he has to marry you!

Always act as if everything's great,
even if you're on the verge of
getting fired.

If a man asks if you're having
a good time, simply say 'yes'
and smile.

Don't call him and rarely
return his calls.

If you're desperate to hear his sexy voice – call his answer machine while he's at work and hang up before the beep!

If you meet a man professionally
you still have to do the Rules...

It is up to him to suggest anything else beyond business.

Don't ask a man to dance – wait
for him to notice you and ask you.

If you never meet men accidentally,
try going to dances, tennis parties
or Club Med.

Looking at a man first is a dead giveaway of interest. Let him look at **you**!

On a first date, avoid staring romantically into his eyes – he will know you are planning the honeymoon!

Don't gaze at a man too much –
he will feel crowded and
self-conscious.

If you don't know what to say on a date, just listen to what he says and follow his lead.

Men feel good when they work hard
to see you. Let them!

Be quiet and reserved on a date –
he'll think you're interesting and
mysterious!

Don't meet him halfway for a date –
make the place of meeting
convenient to you.

Don't go Dutch on a date.
Why deprive him of the joy of
feeling chivalrous?

Do the Rules and he will think
you're the sexiest woman alive!

Always end the phone
call first. Say:

~♡~

☆ 'I have a million things to do'

☆ 'Well, it's been nice talking to you'

☆ 'Actually, I'm kind of busy right now'

Don't stay on the phone for longer than ten minutes. Buy a timer if you have to!

Be friendly, light and breezy on
the phone.

If you're home on a Friday night,
leave the answer machine on.
Always let him think you are out
having a good time.

Never let him think you are at home
thinking about him and making the
wedding guest list.

Don't accept a
Saturday night date
after Wednesday.

Fill up your time before a date so you don't get nervous and anxious.

If your mother can't wait for you
to get married, don't see her before
a date. It might make you reek of
her desperation.

Don't let him catch you writing
your name and his in different
combinations.

Good topics when you start dating
are books and films – not marriage,
kids, love and sexual positions.

Always give the impression you are busy and sought after by other men.

Don't tell a man what a mess you were in before you met him.

Don't tell him what your hairdresser
thinks about your relationship.

Don't give him the third degree
about his past relationships.

Don't say 'We've got to talk' in a serious tone.

Don't overwhelm him with your
career triumphs.

Don't plague him with your
neuroses!

Always end a date first.
Say: 'Gosh, I really must be going
now. I have such a busy
day tomorrow.'

Never tell a man what to do.

♡

Rules for dating in
school...

☆ don't act like one of the boys

☆ act confident even if you don't
feel it

☆ take up sport

Stop dating a man if he doesn't buy you a romantic gift for your birthday or Valentine's Day.

Be aware that men fall in love faster than women. They also fall **out** of love faster.

At the end of a first date, only allow
a light peck on the cheek or lips
even if you're dying to do more.

Don't rush into sex – just think how much passion will have built up by the time you actually say YES!

Don't be a drill sergeant in the bedroom – relax and let him explore your body like uncharted territory.

After great sex, don't say: 'Do you want me to make room in the wardrobe for your clothes?'

After a passionate night together, don't suggest coffee and croissants in bed to prolong your time with him. It might make him run to the nearest greasy spoon café for breakfast!

If you don't plan to sleep with a man for a while, let him know. Don't let him think you're a tease.

Always use a condom. Remember, you're a Rules girl and you take good care of yourself.

♡

Don't expect a man to change or try to change him.

Rules for dating in
university...

☆ don't follow him around campus
in the hope he will notice you

☆ get involved in extra-curricular
activities study – smart is sexy!

Don't throw out his favourite but
disgusting old jeans.

Dating is like slow dancing, so you must let the man take the lead.

The man must be the first person
to say 'I love you.'

♡

Let him introduce you to his
friends before you introduce him
to yours.

Be discreet about a new relationship. You don't want your friend saying: 'Oh it's nice to meet you. Sheila has told me so much about you.'

Dating is not therapy. Don't get heavy in an attempt to bond with him.

Rules for writing or
answering a personal
ad...

☆ keep it short, upbeat and flirtatious

☆ accentuate the positive

☆ don't mention marriage or kids

Don't listen to your answer machine
when he is in your home.

Don't sign him up for career counselling because **you're** unhappy with his current job.

Hide this book, or any other
self-help guides from him.

Don't use words such as 'nurturing', 'relationship' or 'bonding'. You don't want to sound like a walking relationship book.

If you want commitment and are not getting it, be just a little distant and difficult. Men often propose when they are afraid of losing you.

Act independent ... always be
coming or going.

Rules for office dating:

~ ♡ ~

☆ don't have lunch together

☆ don't spy on him or ask his
secretary who called

☆ be professional – don't kiss or hold
hands at the office.

Don't invade his space.

Even if you're married or engaged,
you still need the Rules.

Should you live with a man if you haven't set a wedding date?

Yes, but only if he wants to and you don't!

To recapture a man's interest, dress sexier. No man likes coming home to a woman wearing sweatpants all the time.

Men are often flattered if they are asked out by women ... but these are not the women they end up marrying or dating.

How do you know if a man is attracted to you? He will he find ways – excuses – to be near you.

If you have to call a man and remind him you exist, something is wrong.

If a man doesn't call, don't waste time analyzing what you may have done wrong.

Don't tell a man your life story
too soon.

Excuses a woman
makes to herself to call
a man – but shouldn't!

~♡~

☆ you think he lost your number

☆ you think he thinks you're not interested

☆ your friend says: 'Call him, it's the 1990s'

Your first date with an ex-boyfriend
is like a first date with a man
you've just met ... you must do
the Rules.

Don't waste time on fantasy relationships – with your handsome doctor, accountant or broker. Save yourself for the real thing.

♡

Rules girls know they are either dating a man or not. There's nothing in between.

Can you turn a friend into a boyfriend? Only if he's always really liked you but circumstances have prevented things going any further.

To find out if a man is really interested in you, don't accept last-minute dates. If he likes you, he will keep asking.

Don't cancel everything you normally do at the weekend so you can spend every minute with your man.

Remember, it is better to date no one than to date or marry Mr Wrong.

If nothing is happening on the man front, finish the novel you started writing, redecorate, or find a new hobby.

Be aware that if something doesn't feel right in your relationship, it probably isn't.

Don't get too emotionally involved
too quickly.

Rules for married
women:

~♡~

☆ look the best you can

☆ don't be a nag

☆ pretend you're dating him all
over again

Dating a married man is like driving
down a dead-end street – it gets
you nowhere.

If you do date a married man, make sure he is at least separated from his wife.

Don't wait indefinitely for a man to sort out his life.

Don't be jealous if he has children
and puts them before you.

Don't get too emotionally involved
too quickly.

Always give the impression you are busy and sought after by other men.

Fill up your time before a date.
Be busy so that when the doorbell
rings you're breathless and
brimming with energy.

Make sure the message you record on your answering machine is in good taste, not outlandish.

Why you should **not** discuss the Rules with your therapist:

☆ she might think they are dishonest
and manipulative

☆ she might try to talk you out of
doing it

☆ she doesn't realize you **have** to
do the Rules to find Mr Right

Don't read self-help books that encourage you to pursue men.

If you're on the phone and he calls on the other line, do not get off the phone every time for him.

If you have been
dumped...

☆ don't write pleading letters offering to change

☆ put on a sexy dress and go to the very next party

☆ say to yourself: 'his loss!'

Remember to say 'please' and 'thank you' on dates. Rules girls are a refreshing breed – they're polite.

If he's dating others, you should date others as well.

The first or second date can be on a week night. But the third date **should** be a Saturday night.

Never tell a man you are doing
the Rules.

Don't send a man brochures or newspaper clippings that you think he'd be interested in. Men can find this kind of attention too intense.

Never show a man that you are jealous or insecure.

If he calls you, he likes you. If he doesn't, **Next!**

♡

Let his object in life be to win
you over.

More excuses a woman makes to herself to call a man – but shouldn't!

✩ you want to ask him why he
didn't call

✩ you're just calling to say 'hi'

✩ he said: 'Call me'

When he asks you out, silently count to five before saying yes. It will make him nervous, which is a good thing.

Even though you are hard to get,
make sure you are easy company
to be with.

When walking down the street, drop **his** hand first, ever so slightly.

Don't forget to practise the Rules.
The more you practise, the easier
it gets.

Do the Rules even when your friends and parents think it's nuts.

If you are unsure about him, double-date with a Rules-minded friend. She will tell you whether he's planning to marry you or not.

If you think you're too smart for the
Rules, ask yourself:
'Am I married?

...If not, why not?!'

9 reasons why you
should do the Rules:

1) he will watch out for you

2) he will **listen** when you talk to him

3) he will call to see how your doctor's visit went

4) he will write you love notes
or poetry

5) he will give you little presents
on every possible occasion

6) he will always be ready to make
up after a fight

7) he won't work late because he will want to see more of you

8) your picture will be in his wallet

9) he will be desperate to marry you!

DO THE RULES AND LIVE HAPPILY EVER AFTER... !